Thanksgiving Day

Dorothy Goeller

Bailey Books
an imprint of
Enslow Publishers, Inc.
40 Industrial Road
Box 398
Berkeley Heights, NJ 07922
USA
http://www.enslow.com

Bailey Books, an imprint of Enslow Publishers, Inc.

Library of Congress Cataloging-in-Publication Data

Goeller, Dorothy.
Thanksgiving day / Dorothy Goeller.
p. cm. — (All about holidays)
Summary: "Simple text and photographs present a story with a Thanksgiving theme"
—Provided by publisher.
  ISBN 978-0-7660-3809-7
1. Thanksgiving Day—Juvenile literature. I. Title.
GT4975.G64 2011
394.2649—dc22   2010012567
Paperback ISBN: 978-1-59845-178-8

Printed in the United States of America

062010 Lake Book Manufacturing, Inc., Melrose Park, IL

10 9 8 7 6 5 4 3 2 1

To Our Readers: We have done our best to make sure all Internet Addresses in this book were active and appropriate when we went to press. However, the author and the publisher have no control over and assume no liability for the material available on those Internet sites or on other Web sites they may link to. Any comments or suggestions can be sent by e-mail to comments@enslow.com or to the address on the back cover.

✪ Enslow Publishers, Inc., is committed to printing our books on recycled paper. The paper in every book contains 10% to 30% post-consumer waste (PCW). The cover board on the outside of each book contains 100% PCW. Our goal is to do our part to help young people and the environment too!

Photo Credits: Shutterstock.com

Cover Photo: Shutterstock.com

Note to Parents and Teachers

Help pre-readers get a jumpstart on reading. These lively stories introduce simple concepts with repetition of words and short simple sentences. Photos and illustrations fill the pages with color and effectively enhance the text. Free Educator Guides are available for this series at www.enslow.com. Search for the *All About Holidays* series name.

Contents

Words to Know 3

Story 4

Read More. 24

Web Sites 24

Index 24

Words to Know

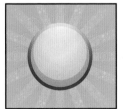  

sun　　　　**turkey**　　　　**turkeys**

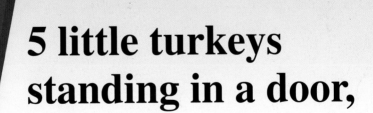

5 little turkeys standing in a door,

One ran off.

Now there are 4.

4 little turkeys under a tree,

One ran off.

Now there are 3.

3 little turkeys with nothing to do.

One ran off.

Now there are 2.

**2 little turkeys
stand in the sun.**

One ran off.

Now there is 1.

1 little turkey better
run away,

because today is
Thanksgiving Day.

Read More

————, *Over the River: A Turkey's Tale*. New York: Simon & Schuster Children's Publishing, 2005.

dePaola, Tomie. *My First Thanksgiving*. Grosset & Dunlap: New York, 2008.

Web Sites

Kids Table Games. *Best-Ever Thanksgiving.* <familyfun.go.com/thanksgiving/thanksgiving-kids-table-fun>

Thanksgiving Games. *Online Games, Coloring Printables, and Thanksgiving activities.* <holidays.kaboose.com/thanks-games.html>

Index

door, 5

sun, 17

Thanksgiving, 23

tree, 9

turkey, 21

turkeys, 5, 9, 13, 17

Guided Reading Level: B
Guided Reading Leveling System is based on the guidelines recommended by Fountas and Pinnell.

Word Count: 66